Hook, I
& Stinker

By

Gary Rowley

Guarantee stamp designed by Starline / Freepik
Fishing imagery designed by Bimbimkha / Freepik

If you need fishing puns, here's some *Gudgeons*!

Climb aboard, if you dare, for a side-splitting voyage of mayhem, mirth and merriment, courtesy of Hook, Line & Stinker, overflowing with 100s of original fishing jokes, puns and one liners.

The must-have companion for all anglers, you'll discover rivers of good, clean fun, ammunition aplenty to unleash an endless tirade of torture and torment upon fellow fishermen, family and friends.

Victims will be at sea, steaming for port, desperately trying to fathom the source of the onslaught, blissfully unaware it's merely the calm before the storm. And all you'll need to do to continue the punishment is sit back, relax, and slowly turn the page...

Let *Minnow* how you get on - enjoy!

Dedicated to Jerry B, Johnny Walker, Adam, Alex & Bonesey – aka the Eagles!

If you need any fishing puns, give me a shout…I've got some *Gudgeons*!

I overlaid for my sea fishing trip and missed the boat. Big missed hake…huge!

That's the last time I'll ask the missus to fetch me a pint of casters. She arrived home with a beer glass filled with bed wheels.

So I said, a pint of maggots, please. Assistant said, sorry, sir, but we don't have any maggots. I said, I'll have a pint of casters, then. Assistant said, I'm afraid we don't have any casters, either. I said, right, I'm putting a complaint in. What's the name of this place, anyway? He said, Marks and Spencer Food Hall, sir…

I don't think the bloke at the tackle shop quite got it when I asked for ten per cent off. He charged me full price for one thing. Then, when I got home, I realised my ten-foot feeder rod was now a nine-foot feeder rod.

She said, surely you're not going fishing in this lot? It's raining cats and dogs. I said, tell me about it. Look at all those flipping poodles…

I used to be addicted to wet weather fishing. But I'm happy to say I've been dry for a couple of years now.

Count Dracula, fishing. I said, any bites, mate? He said, what do you think…?

I've booked a fishing trip to the Far East. Cleethorpes, here I come!

My fishing nickname is 007. 0 bites. 0 fish. 7 hours.

I went on a fishing trip to Ireland. This bloke said, what do you think to County Down, then? I said, to be honest, it's not been half as good since Carol Vorderman left.

I bumped into my mate on his way fishing. I said, off anywhere nice? He said, just a few hours on the bank. He wasn't kidding, either. I saw him again ten minutes later, setting up on Barclays rooftop.

This sign on the tackle shop counter said: Manager's Special. I thought, yeah, right...perhaps in your eyes.

Alien walks in a tackle shop and buys a spool of mainline. Then says, take me to your leader...

I've just been told they're fetching out maggot flavoured crisps. I'm waiting with baited breath.

Bloke asks for a pint of mix-maggots. Assistant says, if you want a pint of Mick's maggots, pal, I suggest you check with Mick first...

This fisherman asked if I could recommend the best place for leads. I said, have you tried Pets at Home...?

I asked a bloke dressed as a crab to lend me a tenner. Come on, I said...don't be so shellfish.

Two pals, lost on a fishing trip to Scotland. One says, there's still no sign of the Forth Road Bridge. Other replies, I'm not surprised. We haven't been over the other three yet.

I showed the missus my new reel. She said, fightin drag! I said, no, but it's got a brilliant retrieve. She said, fightin drag! I said, no, but it's got super slow oscillation. She said, fightin drag! I said, what *are* you talking about? She said, two female impersonators, having a scrap in the street!

I grabbed my rod holdall then had a walk up to the reservoir in a suit of armour. Don't you just love a spot of knight fishing...?

The missus ordered me a whip online. I haven't got the heart to tell her you can't catch fish with a cat o' nine tails.

I was asked to submit a fishing article for online discussion. Unfortunately, I'd nothing forum...

The bloke who built the canal bridge...you wouldn't want to cross him.

I went to A&E with a cut on my arm. Quack said, is there any fish in it...?

All this hype about plastic banknotes lasting longer than paper ones is complete hogwash. A packet of hooks and a pint of maggots and that was a fiver gone already.

The wife resigned her position at the car hooter factory to start work on a maggot farm. I don't know why she bothered to be fair. The money's the same and she's still honking.

Our kid arrived home with his hair cut into the shape of a common sea fish. I don't think the barber fully understood when he said he wanted a mullet.

Someone said there was a barbeque at the fishery. When I got there, it was loads of men, waiting for a haircut.

I hired a river fish costume for a fancy dress party, then got all stressed when it was time to go for the bus. The wife told me not to fret. She said it was understandable I was feeling a bit tench.

The new fishery that's opened. There's a carp lake, a coarse lake and another filled with old socks...which I can only assume is the stocking pond.

I haven't caught a fish for nearly a year now. On a more positive note, at least I'm doing my bit for the planet. I'm the only angler in the club who can categorically state he's net zero.

My new bait boat broke down first time out. Built in Antenna, it says on the box. It's the last time you'll catch me buying any foreign muck, I can tell you.

I didn't think much to the new tackle shop. It was full of footballers, sliding around and kicking lumps out of one another.

Those new-fangled fish finders are a bit too sensitive for my liking. I took mine in Aldi and ended up cleaning them out of frozen cod and haddock.

I rang the shop. I said, I left a pole for elastication. Can you tell me how long it will be? He said, last time I checked, pal, it was still twelve and a half metres.

I accidentally set fire to my fishing jacket...now it's a blazer.

I set fire to my fishing trousers next. Great news...I've always fancied a pair of flares.

There's a bloke on our street that collects waterproof fishing garments. What an anorak.

Angler jumps in the lake with a bar of soap. Bailiff says, hoy, what's going on, like? He says, calm down, mate. I'm just doing what it says on the back of my breakfast mushrooms...washing before use.

The army carp angling team turned up at the fishery and jumped straight in the water. It was all the CO's fault. He was the one who told them to fall in.

No wonder I can't afford to go fishing anymore. Two thousand pounds it cost to fill the tank up yesterday. Honestly, I rue the day I ever laid eyes on that army surplus Challenger 2.

My new pole came with two scraggy tortoiseshells and a ginger tom. Whey hey, I thought...three spare kits.

Considering taking up match fishing, I popped down to the tackle shop. Assistant said, the first thing you'll need is a Seat Box. I said, if that's the case, count me out. I bought a Seat Leon once. It was crap on petrol and all it did was break down on me.

I posted a series of inflammatory remarks on a sea fishing forum. Now I'm in Facebook jail...accused of online trolling.

What would you get if you crossed a Star Wars villain with a pair of salopettes? Darth Wader.

Boy: dad, dad, there's a man at the door, collecting for the local fishery. Dad: well, don't just stand there...get him a bucket of water.

I went in Burger King and asked for two whoppers. Assistant said, you don't half look like Brad Pitt...and the lads at the fishing club say it's only a matter of time before you're picked for England.

Angler goes to the bookies and asks for the odds on finding a dragon, nesting on the fishery. Cashier says, sorry, sir, but dragons are mythical creatures, so it's impossible to process your request. He says, alright, what's the odds on me winning FishOMania? Cashier says, and what colour dragon would that be, sir...?

Fast asleep on my new bedchair, I dreamt I was eating a giant marshmallow. When I woke, my pillow had gone.

The bloke who invented match fishing. Word has it is he's pegged it.

My first attempt at match fishing went brilliant. I caught a box of England's Glory and two boxes of Swan Vestas.

I went to buy a new reel. I said, I'd like one with two concertos by an 18th Century German-British composer. Assistant said, sorry, sir, but I'm afraid we're clean out of double Handels.

I opened my Christmas present from the wife. I said, a box of Kellogg's cornflakes? I said sea reel…not cereal.

Richard Branson has put a bid in for our local tackle shop. Apparently his nephew wants a cowboy outfit for Christmas.

This bloke asked if I fancied donating to a fishing match for Charity. I said, do I heckers like…those Emmerdale Dingles earn far too much as it is.

If I told you a joke about fishing towels…would you say I had a dry sense of humour?

We were enjoying a bankside brew when the cry went up, twit-twoo, twit-twoo. So I said, right, what's the most common owl in Great Britain? He said, is it a barn owl? I said, nope. He said, tawny owl, then? I said, nope again. In actual fact, it's a tea towel…

Our kid bought twenty pairs of jeans from the charity shop and immediately started tearing the zippers out. He said, before anyone asks, I'm taking up game fishing and I've been told to make sure I take plenty of flies.

World hide and seek champion goes to buy a packet of hooks. Assistant says, eyed? They found him four hours later, skulking behind a pile of boxes in the warehouse.

I phoned the angler's association. They asked me to hold the line…

It was my big speech at the angling club AGM. I said, they're small and minty and keep my breath really fresh. And the cry went up, whoa, whoa, it's tactics we're interested in, pal…not tic tacs.

Just my luck. I won a wok in the carp society raffle, but hate Chinese food. Not to worry…I've put that much weight on lately, I can always use it to iron my shirts in.

Speaking of which, I fell downstairs last night and the missus swore blind it was EastEnders going off…

If you receive any emails about half price luncheon meat, ignore it…it's Spam.

Millionaire in a tackle shop, talking pole problems. Assistant says, have you thought about buying a new roller? He says, a new Roller? Not likely…I've just spent a hundred grand on a Bentley convertible.

Two fish doing a crossword. One says, six across: temporal, frontal and parietal lobe? Other says, what do you think I am, like…a brain sturgeon?

Bloke turns up at the fishery with a vicar under his arm and immediately starts bashing a trout over the head with him. No, no, no, came the cry…I said a *priest*!

My mate got that job in the tackle shop returns department. Seriously, I take it all back…

I wonder why so many people get eaten by sharks? I mean, you'd think they'd make themselves scarce once they heard the music, wouldn't you?

My three favourite things are hand feeding sharks my family and not using commas.

Two anglers walk into a fishing lodge. You'd have thought at least one of them would have seen it, wouldn't you…?

The girlfriend dumped me on account of my obsession with angling. Not to worry…I suppose there's plenty more fish in the sea.

Window cleaner buys a sea rod, sea reel, hooks and line. Assistant says, if you're needing bait, a bit of rag usually does the trick. He says, brilliant news…I've got tons in my bucket.

I called the wife and asked if she wanted me to pick up Cod and Chips on the way home. She said it was the worst mistake of her life, letting me name the twins…

This sea angler told me he was naming his new born twins, Haddock and Halibut. I thought, what a load of pollocks...

1st Fisherman: I'm blooming starving. I wonder if the local curry house does takeaways? 2nd Fisherman: I've no idea...but if they do, like, will you ask them what 857,357 – 539,938 is? I've got my daughter on the phone, needing help with her maths homework.

A set of storeroom rods, having an argument with a set of storeroom reels about who was best at arithmetic. Rod says, right then, what's 8,923 times 7,998? Reel says, 71,366,154. Rod says, that's cheating...you're a multiplier.

I didn't get that job at the fishmongers. I'm absolutely gutted.

I was queuing up in the fishmongers when trading standards burst in. The boss man shouted, you behind the counter...don't move a mussel.

This bloke threatened to beat me unconscious with a wet fish. I said, stop talking codswallop.

I wasn't happy when I discovered Facebook was down. I had to ring eighty-six people to see how many fish they'd caught.

I swapped my laptop for a Mac. Granted, I can't get on the internet anymore...but it doesn't half keep me dry when I'm out fishing.

First day at the tackle shop, I took delivery of a roll of bubble-wrap. I said, what shall I do with this, Gaffer. He said, take it in the stores and pop it in a corner. Six hours later, I was still there…pop, pop, pop.

Fluff chucker, boasting how many game fishing records he held. I thought, yeah, right…somehow I trout it.

I went cold weather fishing with a painter and decorator. Never again, I can tell you. I got sick of him telling me I needed two coats on.

Boxer goes in a tackle shop and asks for a pair of forceps. Assistant says, straight-nosed? He says, you trying to be funny…?

I was telling my mate how I was sitting in my car, checking my reel lines, when this van crashed into me from behind. He said, bit of whiplash, was it? I said, actually, no…it was two hundred yards of eight pound Maxima.

What would you get if you crossed an infamous, 19th century serial killer with a herring? Jack the Kipper.

I've just downloaded an album by my favourite underwater pop duo. Don't you just love Pike and Tuna Turbot?

A label on my new fishing trousers said, 32 leg. I thought, crikey, that would fit four octopuses.

I borrowed a fiver off my mate, then a pound straight after. I paid him back a few days later with an off-colour, ink squirting, soft bodied, eight armed, tentacled mollusc that some people prefer to call calamari. I said, there you go, pal…there's that sick squid I owe you.

Two cannibals, sea fishing. One says, three hours now and we've not had a bite. How about we eat a fisherman for dinner and then use his ears as bait? Other says, brilliant idea. I've heard the fish round here are partial to a bit of lug…

I'm desperate to tell the world I'm self-identifying as an ornamental carp. I just daren't. Don't ask me why…I'm not usually so koi.

I went to the pet shop. I said, I'd like to buy a koi carp. Assistant said, would you like an Aquarium? I said, I don't care what star sign it is.

A mate of mine has rented the village hall to give a talk on fish gutting techniques. Daft lad, he'll never fillet…

I'll swear I'm turning into a shark. I'm going fin on top.

I saw a great white, handing over dosh on a doorstep. Ooh look, I thought…a loan shark.

Did you hear about the bloke who thought Salford Van Hire was a Dutch international match angler?

I watched this fantastic film last night about a whale called Moby Dick. It was so good, in fact, I might nip down to WH Smith's later and see if the book is out yet.

I've just bumped into Captain Ahab and he had a runny nose. I said, get whale soon.

I bought some fishing trousers in a 50% off sale. I only got one leg.

So there I was, enjoying a relaxing afternoon's fishing, when the wife rang to tell me the computer had crashed. I said, crashed…? I didn't even know it had sent off for its licence.

My new job, fitting line slowing features to fishing reels, isn't quite what I expected. In actual fact, it's a bit of a drag…

So I said, doctor, doctor, I keep thinking I'm sharing a bivvy with my mirror image. Quack says, you know your trouble, don't you…? You're two in tents.

Bloke goes into a tackle shop and says, got any size 16 elastic, mate? Assistant says, Holler? He says, GOT ANY SIZE 16 ELASTIC, MATE!

These stories about me booking a fishing trip to the Indian Ocean, don't believe a word…they're nothing but Mauritius rumours.

So I said, what's the fastest thing underwater? He said, a motor pike and side carp? I said, actually, I think you'll find it's a Russian built, rocket powered, VA-111 Shkval, super-cavitation torpedo.

What did the fish say when it swam into a concrete wall? Dam!

I went fishing with a dentist. He bagged a brace.

What did the fishing mad dentist type into his sat nav? Route: canal.

It's been announced the chap who invented bait pumps has died. I filled up when I found out…

Bloke turns up at the fishery with a satchel filled with maggots and casters. Mate says, I said cool bag…not school bag.

I had a brilliant evening at Wigan Casino, then finished the night off with a flat fish supper. You can't beat a bit of northern sole.

With a minute to go in the fancy dress fishing match, an angler dressed as a chicken was vying for top spot with another dressed as an egg. I thought, hmmm…now this *is* going to be interesting.

This bloke asked me what my record barbel was. I said, I once spent four quid on a pint of Guinness. Other than that, I'm teetotal…

I'm well impressed with commercial fishing. First time out and I netted adverts for Amazon, T-Mobile, and another with some German geezer going on about Vorsprung durch Technik…

The missus bought me a bait fridge for my birthday. You should have seen my face light up when I opened it.

I'm sick of hearing how fishing lines are overrated. Well, so is my new bait…three weeks I've been using it now and I've not had a bite.

My pal's invited me to enrol at his favourite carp fishing venue. By all accounts, it's run by two lovely ladies…one called Cindy…and another called Kate.

I met the missus on a website for dolphin impersonators…we just clicked.

I opened a shelter for abandoned dolphins. All was going well until some jobsworth from the council said it wasn't fit for porpoise.

I've just seen a shoal of yellow dolphins in Asda. Bless her heart, the missus swore blind it was a bunch of bananas…

Bloke goes in a tackle shop and makes a noise like a donkey. Assistant said, braid it is, sir. Any particular brand…? So he woofed like a dog and the assistant reached for a spool of Berkeley. Then he made a noise like a chicken. Assistant said, I'm afraid you've lost me this time. Why a noise like a chicken? He said, because I can't make a noise like a Shimano Aerlex seven-thousand size spodding reel…

So I said to this butcher on the next peg; I said, good luck, old pal…tight loins.

I phoned the tackle shop. I said, can you recommend a good large arbour? He said, I've heard Singapore's not bad.

Sea angler arrives at the surgery and dumps a ton of wet fish on the doorstep. Receptionist says, er, I think you'll find this is the doc's…not the docks.

I told my mate I was thinking of starting a wet fish business. He said, sole trader? I said, I was thinking more cod and haddock, actually.

Fishing rod walks into a pub. Barman says, what kind of rod are you, like? Fishing rod says, me…? I'm a Shakespeare. He says, you're Bard.

The rumour that's been going around that the fishing club's bank account has slipped into the red. Don't quote me, like…but I think there might be something in it.

Two pals, fishing near a bridge. Suddenly, a funeral cortege passes over and one of the men stands up and takes his cap off, bowing his head. When the cars have gone, he puts his cap back on, sits back down and carries on fishing. His mate turns to him and says, do you know, that's one of the most respectful things I've ever seen. He says, well, we were married for nearly thirty years…

I bought a second-hand hearse to replace my old fishing van and thought I'd put it through its paces on the M1. Just my luck, I got a ticket for undertaking.

So there I was, maggot drowning, when this bloke drifted past with a polling card in his top pocket. Ooh look, I thought…a floating voter.

I took my bite alarms back to the shop. I said, I want my money back. Three weeks I've had these and they haven't gone off once.

I bought a set of Hokey Cokey bite alarms, but wish I hadn't bothered. It takes me three hours to get out of my sleeping bag.

Fitting a motion detector in the lodge toilet wasn't the best of ideas. Every time someone does a jobbie, the flipping alarm goes off…

I opened the toilet door and discovered the bailiff, fast asleep on the pot. Apparently he was having a day in loo he'd been promised.

Historians have discovered the headstone of the world's oldest fisherman on a stone plaque in the gateway to a Sheffield fishery. Apparently he was 162 and his name was Miles from London.

I bought a new feeder rod and was given a copy of Racing Post, with red circles drawn around horses in the 1.45, 2.30 and 3.25 races at Haydock Park. I said, no one mentioned it came with three tips.

This bloke asked what the biggest fish I'd ever caught was. I said, twenty-two inches. He said, that's not very big, is it? I said, that's between the eyes…

So I said, I lost a 37lb carp today. He said, how did you know how much it weighed if you lost it? I said, it had scales on its back.

This match-man asked my advice about pole elastication problems. I said, have you thought about a bung? He said, I haven't, actually. What do you say? Will a couple of hundred do it…?

I've just had the police round, saying my dog was chasing a bloke with a fishing rod. I said, it couldn't have been my dog…it hasn't even got a fishing rod.

Sales rep arrives home with a fully erected bivvy on his car roof. Missus says, what's all this about? He says, it's that new micro-managing gaffer, isn't it? He's only gone and had a Trakker fitted…

I said, next time I go fishing, I'm definitely taking a paperback with me. The chap on the next peg was mesmerised by a book by some geezer called Joseph Heller. She said, Catch 22? I said, did I heck…I blanked again, same as last week.

Two tackle shop employees, having a right old ding-dong. One says, and what do you think miladdo will have to say when he finds his winter skin hasn't been delivered? Other replies, I dread to think…all I know is I'm not taking the wrap for it.

So I said, I caught a forty-pound carp last week. He said, not bad. Any witnesses? I said, of course…or it would have been sixty-pounds.

All I got for winning my section was a picture of Spanish opera singer, Placido Domingo. I said, is that it…a flipping tenor?

I saw this bloke, hopping repeatedly over a piece of rope on the bridge of a trawler. Ooh look, I thought…the skipper.

My deep sea swim-with-the-fish diving business is in trouble. I'm struggling to keep my head above water…

I arrived at the till with a rod I'd picked. Cashier said, swipe your card, mister. I said, did I heck swipe it. Phone the bank if you like…they'll vouch for me.

I went to catch the bus to go fishing. I said to this pregnant woman, when's it due, like? She said, a week on Monday. I said, sod that for a game of soldiers…I may as well walk.

Carp angler, humping a bivvy, rod holdall, chair, bedchair, carryall, bait boat, retention sling, stove and pan set around the lake. I said, do you want to borrow my barrow, mate? He said, thanks for the offer…but don't you think I've got enough to carry?

So I said, that fall out I had with 'er indoors about my fishing weekends. I did what you said and took her shopping for cheap flights. He said, how did it go, like? I said, put it this way…I've had better visits to the darts shop.

Bailiff, circling the carp lake, shouting, Stanley? Anyone know who Stanley Is? Stanley, where are you? I said, I'm Stanley, mate. What's up? He said, I've just found your knife, pal. While I've got you, I don't suppose you know a bloke called Phillips, do you? I've just found his screwdriver...

My police lady fiancé wasn't happy. She said, since you took up fishing, the spark has totally gone out of our relationship. Then she tasered me!

I'm not happy with my insurance company. They've said if my bivvy gets nicked on my forthcoming France trip, I won't be covered.

En route to a French fishing trip, I didn't know which way to look when I boarded the cross channel ferry and everyone started jeering me. It's the last time you'll catch me on a blooming boos cruise, I can tell you.

I asked my mate how his French fishing trip went. He said, don't even go there...

I went fishing with Arthur Scargill. I've never known anybody manage so many strikes.

Ex-miner goes into a tackle shop. He says, I'm taking up carp fishing and need some reels. Assistant says, big pits, like? He says, I hope you're not taking the Michael...?

Two blokes on the bank. One says, I'm thinking of divorcing the wife. She refuses to speak to me if I tell her I'm going fishing. Other replies, I'd think twice if I was you...women like that are hard to find.

What do you call a fish with no eye? A fsh.

I ordered a fishing first aid kit. I thought I'd treat myself.

Two roach in a net. One says, what do you think to this fishing lark, then? Other replies, it hurts to admit it…but I'm hooked.

When the weatherman said to expect a touch of frost, the last thing I expected was to find David Jason in the next bivvy.

The long range weather forecast predicts no rain for six months. Maybe so…but somehow I drought it.

Fishery notice: due to prolonged drought conditions, it's been decided that only one half of the lake will remain open in order to save water.

I was fishing in between a couple of rugby mad, black pudding and tripe eating geezers with East Yorkshire accents. Just my luck, I thought…neighbours from Hull.

Pet food giant, Spillers, have pulled out of a deal to sponsor our local fishing team. It was decided we'd look a bit daft with WINALOT on our kit.

Discovering the fishery gardener, fast asleep in a drunken stupor, the bailiff confiscated his gin bottle and poured it on the grass. Two minutes later, it was half cut…

It's been reported that fifty per cent of anglers admit to drinking alcohol while fishing. Staggering.

I found a glossy magazine on the bank, containing explicit pictures of Kermit the Frog and Miss Piggy. Ooh look, I thought…frog's porn.

So I said, I want three Baitrunner reels and don't bother charging for the spools. Assistant said, if you want three Baitrunners, sir, you'll have to pay for the spools as well. I said, no I will not. Free spool reels…it says in your advert, look.

I went to the doctors, thinking I was an insomniac bivvy light. He said, don't tell me…you're finding it hard to switch off at night?

Pouring with rain, I could see the bloke on the next peg, eyeing up my water resistant cap. He said, do you know where I can get one of those from? I said, not off the top of my head.

I said, do you have any fly lines? He said, weight forward? So I stuck my chin and thorax on the counter and said, is that any better…?

My mate's given up fishing to satisfy his new girlfriend. She's obviously the one that got her way.

First I saw trout driving a tractor and then a carp milking a cow. Whey hey, I thought…a fish farm.

I was having a proper set to with the bailiff, when this wasp landed on his chin. It didn't sting him, like…I made sure I got it first with a right hook.

Running late for a flatfish themed fancy dress party, I said to the missus, have you seen the time? Come on, look…get your skates on.

Zipping up my bivvy for the night, I remembered I'd forgotten to set record for science fiction thriller, Knowing, starring Nicolas Cage. Not to worry…I don't suppose it's the end of the world, is it?

I took my rod back to the shop when it started singing: Ging gang gooley, gooley, gooley, gooley, watcha. Ging gang goo, ging gang goo. Assistant said, it sounds like a problem with the guides.

Chap from Warsaw, walking circles round the lake, throwing handfuls of Swim Stim into the water. Whey hey, I thought…a baiting Pole.

I ordered a new rod via mail order. I knew it said free carriage…but I didn't half get a shock when it was delivered alongside a 19th Century, two-seater Hansom Cab.

Done fishing for the day, I settled down on my bedchair, got my laptop out and put on the new pirate DVD I'd bought. Shiver me timbers, there wasn't a pirate in sight…it was a blooming cowboy film.

Pirate gets thrown off the fishery for rule-breaking. Bailiff says, you heard…now take your hook!

I delivered three tons of fresh herring to this American warship. By all accounts, it was for the Navy Seals.

I bumped into my fishing pal in the garden centre. He said, I'm having terrible trouble with my pole elastic. I said, have you tried new bushes...? Ten minutes later, I bumped into him again, queuing up at the till with a couple of hydrangeas under his arm.

Alright, so this has nothing to do with fish...but during the same visit, I also bumped into Michael J Fox. Or at least I think it was Michael J Fox. He had his back to the fuchsia.

Oh, and Ronnie O'Sullivan was there as well. He was eyeing up a plant...

Blanked again, I was packing up for the day, when a talking fish stuck its head out of the water and started goading me. I said, I haven't time for this right now...how about I catch you later?

I got a fish hook in my hand and had to go through to A&E. I'm not saying the queues were bad, like...but there was a bloke in front of me with a particularly nasty musket wound.

What do sea monsters have for dinner? Fish and ships.

I spotted a sparrow-hawk, hovering above my swim, reading a bible. Ooh look, I thought...a bird of pray.

I saw this bloke, stealing the syndicate gate. I didn't say anything to him, like...he might have taken a fence.

We were still a few miles from the venue when the car started juddering. My mate said, what gear are you in? I said, same as last weekend…wellies, waterproof suit and a baseball cap.

So I said, right, now I'm double-jabbed, I'm going to treat myself to a new fishing van. He said, Astra Zeneca, like? I said, not a chance…you'll not catch me behind the wheel of a Vauxhall.

I took my girlfriend fishing. Noticing her reaction after walking past the mouth-watering aroma of bacon cooking in the lodge, I decided to treat her. Yup, I walked her past again…

I told the wife I fancied a set of winkle pickers for my birthday. Ah well, I suppose every cloud's got a silver lining…at least I got a decent pair of shoes out of it.

Never, ever hit your keyboard's F1 button. I did and now my living room is swimming in hybrid carp.

I was never much use at fishing, so I turned my hand to cage fighting instead. Just my luck…I got knocked out by a hamster in the first round.

I wonder why carp anglers are obsessed with German fishermen? Every five minutes, they're either going on about Herr rigs or Herr stops.

This Nile perch sent me a pen pal request. I might just drop it a line one day.

This bloke offered me £200 for my record breaking pike. I was about to snap his fingers off…but the pike beat me to it.

I ordered a set of carp rods with Japanese shrink wrap handles. What I got was three Tokyo psychiatrists, covered head to foot in cling-film.

The missus wasn't happy when I told her I'd spent three grand on a carp fishing trip to Thailand. The good news is the swelling is going down now and there's a chance I could be out of hospital before the weekend…

Noddy angler with a rod sticking out of his backside. No, no, no, came the cry. I said bomb rod…not bum rod.

Against my better judgement, I went fishing on our 30th wedding anniversary. Feeling guilty on the way home, I decided to stop off and buy something pearl, though soon wished I hadn't bothered. Talk about ungrateful…imagine, turning your nose up at a buy 2 get 1 free deal on 40w lightbulbs.

I went in this tackle shop. I said, I'm looking for some information on pole pots? Assistant said, do you mean the vile Cambodian dictator or that bloke who won Britain's Got Talent…?

Hook and line in a river. Hook says: cold in here, innit? Line says: I didn't know hooks could talk…

There's only one thing stopping me being picked to fish for England. I'm not good enough.

If fish spend so much time in schools...how come a major part of the curriculum doesn't surround how to stop getting caught so often?

This Sunday sees the long-awaited grudge match between the cartoonists and caricaturists fishing teams. If anyone's interested, the draw is at ten o'clock.

Interesting fact: shark attacks only occur when the victim is wet.

What's yellow and extremely dangerous? A shark in a Bart Simpson costume.

I took my festival winnings to the casino and spent £500 on chips. The chef was still frying at 6 o'clock in the morning.

So I said, what a day. I only pranged the car and trashed our kid's new thousand-pound pole in the boot. He said, crikey, you weren't hurt, were you? I said, not a chance...I locked myself in the cellar.

Apparently there's a bloke going round tackle shops, stealing fishing garments by order of size. A police spokesperson has confirmed he's still at large.

I said, look at that flash sod, loading his fishing gear into the back of a Rolls Royce. He said, oh, him? He's a sailor and works for Cunard. I said, yeah, I work *******
hard as well...but I can't afford a flipping Rolls Royce.

I've bought a fish and fossil fuel powered hybrid car. It's a Turbot diesel.

Whoever nicked the full length mirror from the lodge toilet needs to take a long, hard look at themselves…

I took my bedchair back to the shop after finding piles of chopped wood, sewn into the mattress. Assistant said, hold on, mister…it was you who you insisted upon lumber support.

Lost on Merseyside, I stopped to asked this bloke the way to my venue. He said, leave your keys in the ignition, jump in the boot and you'll be there in ten minutes.

It's just been on the news that police have recovered a large stash of stolen fishing equipment from behind a Liverpool Job Centre. I'm shocked…I didn't even know Liverpool had a Job Centre.

A lorry spilled twenty pallets of Shimano reels in the Toxteth area of Liverpool earlier. Police said the road was closed for nearly two minutes.

Did you know it's against the law to go fishing when it's thundering and lightning in Tasmania? How the heck am I supposed to know when it's thundering and lightning in Tasmania?

I phoned the police after witnessing a gang of balaclavaed sheep, reversing a car through a tackle shop window. I said, you'd better come quick…there's ram raiders at work.

Our local tackle shop is on high alert after the pet shop next door was robbed overnight. Police have found a metal chain, tied around a lamppost. They think it might be a lead.

I started a new job, letting out fishing chalets. I'd only been there ten minutes when a Sioux Indian walked in, carrying a rod holdall. I said, do you have a reservation? He said, no...I live in a council flat in south Manchester.

Sea fishing mad, my mate's only gone and changed his name to Dogfish. Talk about barking.

What Beatles song did the boy octopus sing to the girl octopus? I wanna hold your hand, hand, hand, hand, hand, hand, hand, hand...

I took a set of blanks to the shop. I said, I need some rings for these. Bloke says, try the tackle shop next door...this is the jewellers.

Two blokes, grilling fish in a churchyard. Holy mackerel.

I woke up with a fish on my pillow. It was a bream come true.

I took my winter clothing back to the shop when I discovered a family of wolves asleep in the lining. Assistant said, excuse me, pal...but you did say you wanted lairs.

A Hollywood stuntman won today's fishing match with a record-breaking haul. Seriously, he was on fire...

So there I was, cooking breakfast, when my sleeve up in flames. As if that wasn't bad enough, the police were called and I was arrested for possession of a fire arm.

Did you hear about the fireman who went carp fishing with a pyromaniac? Word is they got on like a bivvy on fire.

I phoned the police. I said, somebody's just nicked my fishing van with all my gear in the back. He said, did you see who it was? I said, no...but I got the registration number.

Be warned there's a fruitcake going from fishery to fishery, terrorising anglers with burning matches. Police fear it's only a matter of time before he strikes again.

I've joined a bunch of fishermen that meet up once a week to discuss the agony of getting pieces of carbon fibre lodged down the back of finger nails. We're what's commonly known as a splinter group.

A dozen fishermen, gathered outside the fishery entrance, all with bulging keepnets. No, no, no, came the shout. I said weigh in...not way in.

Hippopotamus, fishing. Bailiff says, a fishing hippo, eh? We don't get many of those on here. Hippopotamus replies, I'm not surprised...three hours and I still haven't had a bite.

I'm putting money away for a rainy day. Yup, I'm saving up for a new Trakker fishing brolly.

This gender neutral stuff is seriously getting out of hand. First a 2-man bivvy becomes 2-person bivvy. Then a man-bag becomes a person-bag. Now my fishing pal, Guy Chapman, is scared he's going to have to change his name to Person Personperson.

This year's winter league was held exclusively on sand and gravel based pegs. I won it...on aggregate.

What does a gudgeon and a killer whale have in common? Neither has ever auditioned for a part in Coronation Street.

A priest was walking on the beach and came across two men, pulling another man ashore on the end of a rope. He said, that's what I like to see. Man helping fellow man. When he'd gone, one turned to the other and said, seems like a nice bloke...but he doesn't know the first thing about shark fishing.

When I arrived home from fishing, sneezing and blowing, the wife insisted upon rubbing my chest with Vic. I said, no chance...last time I came out in a terrible rash from his stubbly chin.

I took Olympic swimming champion, Adam Peaty, carp fishing. We hadn't even finished setting up, when he dove head first into the lake and began breast stroking to the far bank. I don't think he quite got it when I pointed out his swim...

Erm, whoever nicked an inflatable mattress from my bivvy last night…if I was you, I'd probably lilo a bit.

Patient: I got a terrible reaction from that haemorrhoid cream you prescribed. Doctor: where did you apply it? Patient: in the fishing lodge while we were having breakfast.

Weighed down with fishing gear, I was waiting to cross the road. This bloke said, do you know there's a Zebra crossing down there? I said, well, I hope it's having better luck than I am.

So I said, a proper dark horse won yesterday's fishing match. He said, who was that, like? Old Harold with the gammy leg? I said, no…Black Beauty.

Well I never…so Mr Kipling is a mad keen angler. I bet he's a right old tackle tart.

Newsflash: thieves broke into the local fishing club last night and nicked all the cups. Apparently the canteen lady is livid.

All this talk about the sacrifices the England fishing team made, preparing for the world championships. What do they want, like…a medal?

Fingerless fishing gloves…I can't see the point in them.

I'm sure my fishing pal is having an affair with the missus. He's been proper miserable of late.

Bloke in the next bivvy, struggling to get to sleep. I said, kip on the edge of your bedchair, mate…you'll soon drop off.

I arrived back at my peg, trousers round my ankles, panicking like billy-o. I said, I've just been for a number two and it came out looking like chips. He said, you want to try pulling that string vest up a bit.

So I said, I've invented a fisherman's pen that can write in all weathers. He said, nice…but will it write other words as well?

I watched this angler, smashing his barrow up with a sledgehammer. I thought, he must be off his trolley.

The fishery gardener is over the moon with his new equipment. He says it's cutting hedge…

I always take an empty milk bottle fishing with me…just in case anyone fancies a black coffee.

What's green and invisible? No bivvy.

I said, how come there's a four-legged shovel, chasing birds round the complex? He said, it's the bailiff's cat…he's had it spade.

I've checked my bank account and reckon I've stashed enough dosh to be able to go fishing every day for the rest of my life…just so long as I pop my clogs a week on Sunday.

Bloke arrives on the bank with a bait-box full of mice. He says, right…where's the best place round here for catfish?

Angler, lobbing King Edwards into his swim. I said, you daft apeth…I said spodding, not spudding.

I went to the tackle shop. I said, is mister Ite in? He said, who? I said, mister Ite? Harold? I've got a crack in a pole section and the lads on the bank said Harold Ite would sort it.

Every time I sit on my new chair, the legs start singing Lonely This Christmas. I think it must be the Mud feet.

I phoned the missus. I said, don't waste money buying me a new set of reels for Christmas. I've just found some hidden under a pile of clothes in the bottom of the wardrobe.

No fishing trips for me for a while. I've been admitted to hospital with food poisoning after mistaking a daffodil bulb for an onion. Word is I won't be out till the spring.

Police recovered 146 stolen fishing rods overnight, all with broken top sections. Apparently they were acting on a tip off.

I asked the missus to get me a set of indicators for Christmas. Now I'm the only angler on our syndicate with a pair of flashing orange bulbs strapped to his kit…

How many fishermen does it take to change a lightbulb? Sixteen…but you should see how big it is.

I swatted three flies while fishing yesterday: two males and a female. How did I know which was which? The males were on beer cans…and the female was on the phone.

My new sleeping bag was delivered with jars of basil, oregano, parsley, rosemary and thyme. I thought, nobody told me it was five season.

I took a policeman fishing. Big mistake. I spent all day trying to educate him upon the benefits of catch and release.

What did the plumber say to his wife when she told him it was her or fishing? It's over, Flo…

Two blokes, small boat fishing, when a squall blows up. One says, if it carries on like this, do you think we'll fall out? Other says, will we heckers like fall out…we've been best pals for twenty years!

I went to the post office to renew my fishing licence. On the way out, the manager stopped me and accused me of nicking a book of stamps. I didn't mess about, like…I stuck one on him.

Bloke, sitting on a windowsill, pulling fish out of a muddy puddle. I thought, what a ledge.

First time fishing, I reeled in a rusty door catch. It must have been beginner's lock.

I was given a fishing jigsaw for my birthday. 7 to 8 years it said on the box. Yeah, right…I had it finished twenty minutes.

Those new waders everyone's raving about. Word has it the tape-sealing is faulty. That is, according to a leaked memo…

I came across a talking duck on the canal bank. I said, you're wasted here, talking duck. In actual fact, I saw the perfect job for you in last night's paper: performing duck required at Billy Smart's Circus. And the talking duck said, I'm afraid that's no good to me, mate…I'm a plasterer.

Did you hear about the fisherman who was hit by a tidal wave of tonic water? He was almost Schwepped away.

I went in this book shop. I said, do you have a copy of Tackle Storage Bags by Carrie Hall?

When the missus left, I spent a few days away carp fishing and cried myself to sleep every night. It was only when I got back I realised she'd stuffed my pillow full of onions.

He said, did you know that humans eat more tuna annually than great whites? I said, I should hope they do…I can't remember the last time I had a great white for dinner.

The clairvoyant turned tackle dealer near us…I popped round the shop this morning and there was a sign on the door saying, closed due to unforeseen circumstances.

I went to buy a new fishing jacket. Assistant said, are you a medium? I said, no…but I watched Most Haunted once.

Fishing mad, my mate bought a house on Trent Close in tribute to his favourite venue. Just in case you wondered, I live at 32 Spearmint Rhino Avenue.

I caught this bloke trying to nick my waders. I didn't half give him some wellie.

Question: if I have six rods and the missus sells five, how many do I have left? Answer: twenty-three…I lied about only having six.

I dumped a big pile of exercise books in my swim. I thought I'd have a go at fishing in the margins.

Bloke from Chicago, baiting his swim with dollar bills. I said, alright, who told him fish were partial to a bit of bread?

I've just seen Elvis on the cut, emptying his keepnet. He was returning a zander.

As a morale building exercise, our fishing team visited a local children's home yesterday. It was heart-warming to put a smile on the faces of people who constantly struggle and have virtually no hope…said little Johnny Walker, aged 7.

I went to buy a shelter. I said, I hope it's better than the last one you sold me. It had loads of flaws in the material. Assistant said, how do you mean, loads of floors? It's a one-man bivvy, mate, not a blinking hotel.

So there I was, wondering how I could raise enough money to buy a new set of reels, when I spotted a sign outside a breaker's yard, saying: cash paid for scrap. I went straight inside and said, right then...are we talking gloves or bare knuckle?

I went with my mate to buy a new pole. Assistant said, gobble-gobble, gobble-gobble. And my mate replied, gobble-gobble, gobble-gobble. I think they were talking turkey.

First overnighter of the season and I only went and overlaid. I couldn't move next morning for flipping eggs.

She said, I got a new rod and reel for my husband. I said, well done...sounds an absolute bargain to me.

If you're ever having one of those awful days on the bank...and want to ease the pain...use your finger and write - 2 - 2 + = on your chair arm, pillow, table, whatever...and you'll hear the chorus from Mary Poppins song, Chim Chiminee, Chim Chiminee, Chim Chim Cheree...scary but true.

Alright, so I lost a game of online match fishing to my computer...but it was no competition when it came to a bout of kickboxing, I can tell you.

I went to the doctors. I said, every time I go carp fishing, I get a brew on then take endless pictures of myself beside boiling kettles. He said, it sounds like you've got a selfie steam issue.

Anyone thinking of going swimming with sharks, don't bother. I tried it once and it cost me an arm and a leg.

Deep sea diving, I got straight on the intercom when my leg was bitten off by a shark. This voice said, which one? I said, how am I supposed to know? There's hundreds of them down here!

I was really looking forward to my fishing holiday in East Anglia. Unfortunately, due to an unfortunate spacing error at the travel agents, I've just spent 2 weeks on Norfolk's B roads.

Where do fish go to sleep? On the river bed…yawn!

I went sea fishing on a boat called Noah's Ark. What a waste of time that was. I was only allowed to take two worms.

So I said, doctor, doctor, I'm obsessed with fishing magazines. My garage, spare bedroom, wardrobe and the cupboard under the stairs are all crammed with thousands of copies of Improve Your Coarse Fishing, Angler's Mail and Trout and Salmon. He said, hmmm…it sounds like you've definitely got a few issues.

Angler, drinking PG Tips, listening to another angler, talking about his Mediterranean cruise. Bailiff says, sorry, gents, but there's no brews or holiday talk permitted while fishing. Check your day tickets…it's all in the teas and seas.

The weatherman said it might be cold but, on the other hand, it could also be sunny. So, just to be safe, I went fishing with one glove on and one glove off.

Blimey, it's blowing a gale out there. Anyone who goes fishing in that lot…hats off to them.

I was woken by the sound of a horse, galloping across my bivvy. I thought, oh no…not another flipping night mare.

I went fishing with Arnold Schwarzenegger. Predator hunting, naturally.

Did you hear about the chiropodist turned fisherman who insisted upon using dried foot skin as bait? He'd heard carp were partial to a bit of corn.

And then there was the ornithologist that took up fishing? Every time he got a bird's nest, it made his day.

I've just seen Big Ears, fishing…him and that silly mate of his. Blooming Noddy anglers.

Angler, grinning like a Cheshire cat, having a picture taken with his catch, while all around people were shouting cheese! Cheese! Seconds later, a giant round of cheddar came rolling down the banking and knocked him straight in the shallows.

I went in the lodge and asked how much the beer was. Barman said, three quid a pint or a fiver a pitcher. I said, just give us a pint…forget the photo.

Bloke goes to the zoo. He says to the keeper, how much for a set of big cat testicles? I'm off carp fishing and the bloke down the tackle shop reckons the best bait is tiger nuts.

Tiger arrives on the fishery and says, can I have……a day ticket please? Bailiff says, why the big pause? Tiger throws its feet in the air and says, don't ask me. I was born with them.

What's green and white and sits in a kitchen? A washing machine in a bivvy.

I went sea fishing and broke the anchor. It didn't go down well.

Every time I go fishing, I convince myself I'm going to blank. Then, yesterday, I had a blood test. And guess what…? It came back B-negative.

So I said, this time tomorrow, I'll be on the plane. He said, what, that fishing trip to the Florida Keys you're always going on about? I said, no…I'm taking an inch off the bottom of the front door.

Struggling to fit into my bib and brace, I said, I'm clapping weight on. I'm sure I've got an overactive, erm, erm… He said, thyroid gland? I said, no…knife and fork.

I treated myself to a new fishing polo shirt. It's mint, like…but it didn't half leave a hole in my pocket.

The bloke in the next swim offered me a glass of hedgehog flavoured beer. I said, I can't drink that…it's been spiked.

With no sign of a bite, I snuggled up in my sleeping bag and watched The Exorcist on my iPad. Honestly, it scared me half to death…now I'm worried what will happen if I put it on again.

I've just seen a snake run over by a motorbike on the path up to the fishery. If you don't believe me, here's a picture: $

Eskimo kid asks his mother what's for dinner. She says, Vera Lynn pie, sweetheart. He says, not whale meat again…?

I once spent an entire season, fishing blindfolded. I was in a bit of a dark place at the time.

1st Fisherman: where are you fishing this weekend? 2nd Fisherman: E-I-E-I-O fisheries, same as last week. 1st Fisherman: if you mean farm fisheries, you've spelled it wrong. 2nd Fisherman: have I heckers like. You've heard the song, haven't you? Old MacDonald had a farm, E-I-E-I-O.

Whoever stole 200 cans of Red Bull from the fishing lodge storeroom...I don't know how you can sleep at night.

To celebrate international book week, I took the little one to school dressed as a spod rod. I said, before anyone asks...he's come as page nineteen of a fishing mail order catalogue.

Two carp, bottom feeding, when a boilie appears on a hook. One says, did you order anything online...?

I went to the tackle shop. I said, how much for a new holdall? Assistant said, hard-case, like? I said, don't be daft...I couldn't fight my way out of a paper bag.

Two anglers, setting up. One says, fish and chips I had for dinner and blooming lovely it was. Other says, I had pancakes for dinner and that was blooming lovely as well. I don't think the kids were too impressed, mind...if only someone had told me pancakes was their favourite rabbit.

I'm thinking of putting my collection of John Lennon memorabilia on E-Bay to fund that new 16m pole I'm after. Imagine all the PayPal...

This bloke offered me a packet of size 16 barbless to alter his trousers for him. I thought, that's a turn up for the hooks...

After one glass too many at the fishing club AGM, I finished up breaking my arm in two places. Falling down drunk at the bar and then again outside the chippy...

Overweight after years of lounging around on a seat box, I went to the doctors. He said, don't eat anything fatty. I said, what, burgers and chips and that? He said, no, fatty, don't eat anything...

Just heard the bailiff kicked this bloke off the fishery in stockings and suspenders. All a bit odd, really...I'd have thought he'd have had his wax jacket and waterproof kecks on as usual.

So I said, well, this time next week, I'll be out catching a few rays. He said, couple of weeks in the Mediterranean, is it? I said, actually, no...I've booked a day flatfish fishing off Morecambe Bay.

I woke at 6.00am and crawled out of my bivvy, unable to work out where the sun had gone. Then it dawned on me...

This bloke told me he'd been fishing with John McEnroe. I said, you *cannot* be serious!

I couldn't afford a fortnight's fishing, so I did the next best thing. I went for a week and didn't go to sleep.

With fishing cancelled, I thought I'd make the effort and have a conversation with the wife for once. I couldn't believe it when she told me she didn't work at Woolworth's anymore...

I was offered a job in a tackle shop. Gaffer said, the starting pay is £10 per hour, rising to £20 per hour after six months. I said, I'll start in six months, then...

After blanking for the third time in a row, I went to the lodge and asked for something stiff. The barman poured me a pint of starch.

I ordered an all-day breakfast from the lodge. I started scoffing at 9 o'clock and didn't finish until 5.30.

Bloke in the car park, casting a line into a pothole filled with rainwater. I thought, oh no…not another puddle chucker.

I phoned home after falling in the river. Missus said, I bet you're wringing wet through, aren't you? I said, ringing wet through…? I'm soaked to the blooming skin, that's all.

This carp angler offered to sell me a bedchair for a tenner. I told him I was definitely interested…but I'd like to sleep on it first.

I've just discovered the wife isn't suffering from Tourette's, after all. She's that sick of me going fishing, she really does want me to ****** off!

A sea angler threatened to drown me in a bucket of seawater. I said, yeah, yeah, yeah…whatever floats your boat.

I asked the bailiff if the fishery did cash back. I said, because, if they do, I'd like a refund. I haven't had a single bite all day.

The AA man fishing opposite lost a fish and immediately began crying his eyes out. I thought, he's heading for a breakdown.

I spent the afternoon fishing next to a bloke with a wooden leg called Wilf. I didn't like asking what his other leg was called.

I've just been bitten by a tiger shark off Llandudno. Talk about Welsh rare bite.

So I said, I'd like to introduce my half-sister. He said, different father? I said, no…shark attack.

I went to buy a pair of waders. Assistant said, rubber sole? I said, if I wanted a Beatles album, pal, I'd be in the record shop next door.

Face palm: what do fish eat their dinner with? Their fish fingers.

I fell over on my way fishing. This bloke said, vertigo? I said, not really…the venue's only just round the corner.

Student: I spent my summer holidays at the fishing lakes, miss, shoving bangers up cormorant's backsides. Teacher: do you mean rectum? Student: wrecked 'em? It blew their flipping heads off!

I was asked what kind of music I listened to while fishing? I said, usually something catchy.

The bloke in the next bivvy was blasting out some proper tunes. Eventually, I went over and said, do you have anything by The Doors? He said, just what you see, pal…a table, stove, kettle and toaster.

Angler, bragging he could cast a lead half a mile across the lake, and then get his dog to retrieve it from the opposite bank. I thought, that sounds a bit far-fetched…

I've phoned in sick that many times to go fishing, next time I'm going to have to tell the boss I've snuffed it.

What time is it when an elephant sits on your seat box? Time to get a new seat box.

I subscribed to my local tackle shop's newsletter. Trouble is, every time they send me an email, it comes up as phishing…

John Travolta sent his reels off for servicing. He said they needed a bit of Grease.

I couldn't work out why everyone was using hand held telephones on the road outside the fishery. Then I realised: I was on the ring road.

They say 40 is the new 30. Try telling that to the speed camera on the road to the fishery.

Each day, I peg our kid out with the washing, then pass him his mobile phone so he can decide what fishing tackle he's going to buy next. He absolutely obsessed with on line ordering.

My wife is leaving me on account of my frequent African fishing trips. Kenya believe that? Ghana miss her.

A talking frog hopped out of the water and started flicking through my fishing magazines. All I could hear was, reddit, reddit, reddit...

I've just seen a pony, fishing. It was doing a bit of trotting.

The missus reckons I've three big faults. One, I'm fishing mad. Two, I don't listen. And three, erm...some other nonsense she was going on about.

Bluebottle goes in a tackle shop and slams £50 on the counter. Owner says, don't tell me...you're taking up fly fishing? Bluebottle says, actually, no...I'm after a gift voucher for my second cousin.

I asked the wife to get me a set of carp rods for my birthday. For some reason, she bought me a colonic irrigation kit instead. I told her to stick it where the sun doesn't shine.

I went to the chippy and asked for haddock and chips twice. Fryer said, alright, alright...I heard you the first time.

What do you call a sandal wearing French fisherman? Phillipe Phillope.

I was trying on a pair of field boots. I said, they feel a bit tight to be honest. Assistant said, try them with the tongue out. So I said, I'm athraid th'till a bit on th'tight th'side...

Bloke in a tackle shop, trying out a chair. He said, can I higher it? Assistant said, if you want it, pal, I'm afraid you're going to have to pay cash for it like everyone else.

I ordered a bacon sandwich from the lodge. I said, stick me some tomato sauce on while you're at it. She said, HP? I said, no, thanks...I'll be paying cash if it's all the same with you.

Bailiff said, every night, this moggy does its business on the bank, then digs a hole and buries it. I said, so what? That's what cats do, isn't it? He said, what, with a shovel...?

I took my rod back to the shop. I said, it keeps meowing at me and last night it caught a mouse in the garage. He said, it sounds like a problem with a feral...

I was watching this carp angler, feeding his swim with handfuls of soil. He was obviously doing a bit of ground baiting.

Rolling hills. If ever you're out fishing and see one coming...dive for cover.

Angler breaks down and gets on the phone to his mate, asking for help. He says, I'd love to, pal. But I'm absolutely bagging up here. A few hours later, he was enjoying a celebratory pint in the lodge, when the broken down angler walked in, covered in engine oil, with a pair of jump leads wrapped round his neck. He says, you're not going to start anything, are you...?

I phoned the wife. I said, I've just bagged a fabulous mirror. She said, well make sure you fetch it home with you. It can go on the living room wall for me to do my hair in.

I said, what? No maggots or pinkies? How about squats? He said, plenty of those, pal…in fact, I managed a couple of hundred this morning down the gym.

Two fishermen, checking out a new venue. One says, nice here, isn't it? Look, there's even a flock of cows in the field behind us. Other says, herd of cows, stupid. He says, course I've heard of cows. Like I said, there's a flock of them over there.

I was doing a spot of shore fishing, when this car pulled up and a couple of gangsters jumped out and began Tommy-gunning this orange thing out at sea. Ooh look, I thought…a drive buoy shooting.

Who runs the undersea Mafia? It's Al Caprawn, of course. He's so infamous, in fact, they've even made a film about him…The Codfather.

We were fishing a venue that bordered a golf course. All of a sudden, the shout went up, fore! I said, get down, quick. We dove to the floor and a ball went flying over our heads. As my mate started to get up, I said, stay down…there's three more to come yet.

I was in the tackle shop when a delivery of Dynamite Baits arrived. I said, who's fetched it, like…TNT?

After discovering I was planning to throw a sickie to go fishing with the lads, the gaffer summoned me to his office. He said, if it's true, I'm afraid I'm going to have to let you go. I said, wow, boss, cheers, boss. I always said you were a top geezer…

I went in this chemist. I said, I need something to keep my feet dry while fishing. Assistant said, I'm afraid we don't sell fishing equipment, sir. I said, I find that hard to believe. Absolutely everyone has told me to try Boots.

Just seen an Irish spider, fishing. It was a Paddy-long-legs and it was doing a bit of spinning.

1st Fisherman: the wife's only taken off shopping again, hasn't she? 2nd Fisherman: what a coincidence. So has mine. What do you fancy doing till they get back? 1st Fisherman: I don't know…how does a week's carp fishing in France sound?

I asked for a pint of mixed maggots. Assistant said, I'm afraid we don't do mixed, mate…only reds, whites and bronze.

I arranged to take Harry Potter ice fishing. When he arrived, I was shocked to see he'd fetched a grunting troll with him. I said, did you listen to a single word of what I told you, Harry? I said auger…not ogre.

I decided to have a go at ice fishing. As I drilled a hole, this voice shouted: there's no fish in there. So I drilled another hole, a few yards away, and the voice came again: there's no fish in there. I drilled again and the same voice shouted: there's no fish in there, either. I said, who are you? God? And the voice said: no…I'm the rink manager.

Bivvied up and absolutely starving, I got on the phone to the local pizza shop and ordered a large, stuffed crust Hawaiian. This voice said, do you want that cutting into eight or twelve pieces? I said, best make it eight…I'd never eat twelve.

Our kid's offered to dredge the fishing lake for a hundred nicker. If you ask me, he's getting in way over his head.

I'm not saying our fishing team is rubbish…but we've clubbed together to buy the captain a cigarette lighter on account that he's always losing matches.

Patient: doctor, doctor, I keep thinking I'm fishing a big Parisian river. Quack: you're in Seine.

When I got my new waders home, I found signed pictures of Richard Gere, Robert Redford and Brad Pitt in the box. So I phoned the shop and said, what's all this about…? I specifically stated I didn't want studs.

My girlfriend finished with me because of my fishing obsession. I still can't believe it…three and a half seasons we've been together.

I received a text, saying the missus was in Casualty. So I rushed home, stuck the telly on and didn't move for an hour. There were plenty of doctors and nurses around...but no sign of 'er indoors. So I got my coat back on and was back at my swim half an hour later.

Southern anglers have been advised to stay indoors as strong winds and blizzards continue to batter the UK. Northern anglers will need their big coats on.

During the recent spell of severe weather, the government advised people to wear hi-vis clothing and carry the following items at all times: blanket, shovel, flask, spare batteries, a jerry-can of petrol, and 72-hours-worth of food and water. Honestly, I felt such an idiot, climbing aboard the number 22 bus...especially when I had to ask the driver to give me a lift with my fishing gear.

Sea angler, dropping sticks of dynamite overboard. Apparently he was trying out a new boom.

1st Fisherman: if I ever win the Lottery, mate, I swear I'll see you right. 2nd Fisherman: do you mean you'll buy me that new Daiwa pole I've been dreaming about? 1st Fisherman: actually, no...what I meant is I'll finally be getting my eyes lasered.

Just my luck, setting up next to some crackpot who thought he was a moth. Two big carp later and with night drawing in, I was relaxing on my bedchair when he stuck his nose through the door of my bivvy. I said, do you realise what time it is? I'm trying to get some shut eye here. He replied, I know and I'm sorry, like. It's just that, well...I saw your light on.

Jealous at how many fish I was landing, this angler threw his cheese sandwich at me. I said, that was mature, wasn't it?

I was on the phone, ordering a new bedchair. I said, do you deliver? He said, if you want liver, pal, I suggest you call the butchers shop next door.

The syndicate flasher has dismissed all talk of retirement. He says he's going to stick it out for at least another couple of years.

I went to the bank to see if I could borrow some cash for a new fishing set up. Cashier said, I'm sorry, sir, but the loan arranger isn't in today. I said, how about Tonto…?

A trio of Irish lumberjacks arrived to do a spot of pruning on the lake. Whey hey, I thought…tree fellers.

I saw this angler on his way into the lodge with a U-Boat under his arm. I said, don't tell me…you're paying your subs.

My set top box lost signal just before the winner of FishOMania was announced. Six hours later and I still don't know who won. Hopefully I'll get a better picture in the morning.

I've just seen a bus, wearing a baseball cap, bib and brace and wellies. I can only surmise it was one of the coaches.

There's a charity fishing match tomorrow in aid of Battersea Dog's Home. Apparently the red hot favourite is some dude called Jack Russell.

I pointed out a rod pod in the tackle shop window. I said, that's the one I'd get. Next thing, Cyclops had me pinned up against a wall. He said, you wanna piece of me...?

Reading the fishing column, I was shocked to see we were top of the league. Then I realised I had my paper upside down.

Did you see last night's documentary about the shipbuilder's fishing team? Riveting.

I went to A&E after picking up a flaming stove instead of my phone. Nurse said, that explains one burned ear. What happened to the other? He said, it rang again a minute later.

So I said, twenty years ago the missus bought me this to keep me warm while fishing, and it still fits me today. He said, mate...it's a blooming scarf.

After a miserable year of blanking, I switched sports and took up blindfold archery instead. If you've never tried it, give it a go...you don't know what you're missing.

I arranged to meet my mate at the fishery. When I got there, he was sat on the loo, trousers round his ankles, casting out a line. I said, no, no, no...I said *carp* fishing.

So I said, a spool of two-pound line, please. Assistant said, if you want a spool of line, pal, you can pay nine ninety-nine for it like everyone else.

Our local fishmonger's been caught selling under-sized shellfish. It will just serve him right if he ends up in the small-clams court.

And then there was the sea angler who dropped his pants, attached a hook and line to his bum-cheek, then stuck his backside in the water. He was doing a bit of bottom fishing.

Announcement: nude charity fishing match next Saturday at 10.00am. Feel free to join us if you've nothing on.

I spent my last tenner on a set of bite alarms with the volume stuck on full. I couldn't turn them down.

There was this bloke, running round the fishing pond, screaming his ear had been chopped off. Is that it? I asked, pointing at the ground. No, he replied, mine had a disgorger on it.

After two days without a bite, I tried feeding my swim with leftover muesli. Seconds later, I fell in and almost drowned. I was sucked under by a strong currant.

The wife says all I do is lounge around, watching old fishing programmes and, if our marriage is to survive, we need to make time to talk. I thought, yeah, right...like that's going to happen when episode one of the second series of River Monsters has just come on.

I've landed a job packing groceries in Tesco. Who says I never bag up?

There's only one thing stopping me being picked to fish for England. I'm not good enough.

I highly recommend those new liquorice flavoured boilies. I caught blooming all sorts.

We had the Beach Boys Appreciation Society fishing team in the lodge last night and they were buying everyone drinks. All you could hear was, round, round, get a round, I get a round…

Two fishermen, discussing fund raising events for the local fishery. One says, how do you fancy running the London Marathon next year? Other replies, don't be stupid…it's brilliantly organised as it is.

This bloke asked if he could have some of my terminal gear. I told him to go and swivel.

Did you hear about the fly fisherman who thought Hip Wader was a country and western singer?

Two parrots on a perch. One says, can you smell fish?

I woke up in my sleeping bag, dressed as a clown. I think I must have slept funny.

Me and the bloke who invented reclining chairs. We don't half go back a long way.

I'm reading a brilliant book entitled, Common Fishing Knots. For anyone interested, it's by a lady called Pat O'Noster.

After my release from prison for handling stolen fishing tackle, I was asked if I'd learned anything. I said, yeah...don't get caught.

What would you get if you crossed a tub of midge larvae with a Batman villain? Bloodworm and Joker.

I didn't half slam the garage door. I said, where's my fly tying equipment gone? She said, your new 2000cc car had the lot for breakfast. And before you start, I did warn you not to buy a tool eater...

This bloke told me he was writing a book on fish. I said, try using paper, mate...you'll find it a lot easier.

Apparently there will be five million UK anglers by 2030. I thought yeah, right...by half past eight tonight?

I had a dream I was angling for 12th century peasants. You can't beat a bit of serf fishing.

I went lure fishing with my mate. Ten minutes in, he'd caught three fish and I hadn't had a single bite, prompting him to check my line for me. He said, there's no wonder you're not catching. You've forgotten to put a plug on it. I said, put a plug on it? No one told me it was electric.

Two fishermen, chewing the fat. One says, every time I bag up, I go home and the wife treats me to a slap up meal. What does your wife do? Other says, I don't know...we've only been married ten years.

Youth goes on the Antiques Roadshow, showing off an antique cane fishing rod. Presenter says: this is worth at least ten thousand pounds. Can I ask where you got it from? Youth says: it was passed down to me, mate. Presenter says: passed down to you from where? Youth says: from this bedroom window, pal...

I only popped out for a pint of maggots and ended up buying a pair of binoculars. I think they saw me coming.

What's green and wears glasses? A bedchair...I was lying about the glasses.

I couldn't believe it when I saw a sign on the lake, saying: please take your litter home. I mean, who in their right mind would take new born kittens fishing with them?

I found a pooch in a bin on the fishery. I said, what's this cocker spaniel doing in here? Dog walker said, it's mine, mate. I was just doing what it says on the sign back there...if your dog has a pooh, pick it up and put it in the bin.

I had a bash at game fishing. I caught a Monopoly, two sets of Ludo and a limited edition Scrabble.

Anybody any idea where Jeopardy is? It says on the front of today's paper that there's a new fifty-acre fishing complex there…

Count Dracula, fishing. Every time a new angler appeared on the lake, his bite alarms went off.

I told my mate I'd been invited to take part in a French fishing match. He said, Toulouse? I said, like heck it is…if I'm going all the way to France, it's to lift the blooming trophy.

I've started work as a waiter in the fishing lodge. Granted, the money's not fantastic…but at least I can put food on the table.

Signing for cardigan factory fishing team was the best move I've ever made. Seriously, we're such a tight knit squad.

What's black, got six legs, wears checked trousers, and could hurt you if it fell out of a tree? Rupert the rod pod.

I went to the doctors, thinking I was a reel handle. He told me I was a total crank.

Sea angler, showing off his prize catch. I said, why the long plaice…?

Two fish in a tank. One says, you drive…I'll man the guns.

Did you hear about the fight at the chippy? Two cod got battered.

Speaking of which, I've just turned down a job at the chippy...I had other fish to fry.

I was offered a litter collecting job at the fishery. I said, will I have to go on any training courses? Bailiff said, no...you'll just pick it up as you go along.

Bloke goes in a tackle shop. He said, I had my best fishing trip ever, but have to say that keepnet you sold me was absolutely useless. Assistant said, but that's the biggest keepnet we have. You can get any amount of fish you like in there. He said, not when you've left it at home in the garage.

After a week away fishing, I decided to book a table for the wife's birthday. What a disaster...she didn't pot a single ball.

One round, one square, one with a lid, one without, plus one each of 17, 13 and 5 litres...and that, ladies and gentlemen, completes my bucket list.

So I said, a pint of maggots, please. He said, maize? I said, I've heard Hampton Court's not a bad one.

Did you hear about the cannibal who went boat fishing, ate his best friend and then regurgitated him into the sea? He brought a whole new meaning to the term, chumming up...

I turned down a job as a lugworm digger. It was a bit beneath me.

My mate jumped at the chance and started last Monday. Honestly, he's as happy as a sand-boy.

So there I was, fast asleep in my bag, when someone started shouting, ready-steady, go! Ready-steady, go! I didn't half wake with a start!

I went for a trial for the local fishing team. Captain said, can you perform under pressure? I said, I don't know the words to be fair...but I do a cracking rendition of Bohemian Rhapsody.

There's a terrible condensation problem in the fishing lodge. If anyone's got any idea what's causing it, please feel free to pop round...the kettle's always on.

I rang home. I said, I'm not saying it's hot here...but you know the plastic surgeon I told you I was fishing next to earlier? Well...he's just melted.

Ok, so I forgot to take my sun tan oil fishing with me and finished up burning my head. There's no need to rub it in...

Last night's fishing drama wasn't the best. In actual fact, the cast was awful.

I got banned off the fishery for telling bad jokes. The bailiff said the rules clearly stated *no corn*.

What would you get if you crossed fishing tackle with a smelly sock? *Hook, line and Stinker!*

If anyone's got anymore decent fishing puns...please let *Minnow*!

If you enjoyed Hook, Line & Stinker, please watch out for further sporty related titles, coming your way soon.

If you can't bear the wait, why not check out the following hilarious publications by Gary Rowley:

That's Terrible! A Cringeworthy Collection of 1001 Really Bad Jokes

That's Terrible 2: A Cringeworthy Collection of 1001 ~~Really Bad~~ Even Worse Jokes

Titanic Book of One Liners

The Daddy

Certified Guaranteed Groans!

All available to purchase on Amazon now!

Printed in Great Britain
by Amazon

14189524R00038